MEMO
OF
SHEFFIELD

PART OF THE TRUE NORTH BOOKS MEMORIES SERIES

First published in Great Britain by True North Books Limited. England HX3 6SN. 01422 244555

Text, design and origination by True North Books
www.truenorthbooks.com

INTRODUCTION

Welcome to Memories of Sheffield, a look back on some of the places, events and people in the city which have shaped the lives of local people over a period of around half a century. The following pages are brought to life by a selection of images from the not-too-distant past, chosen according to their ability to rekindle fond memories of days gone by and show how people used to shop, work and play in the area where they grew up. Modern image reproduction techniques have enabled us to present these pictures in a way rarely seen before, and with this creative pocket sized version we have attempted to set the book apart from some of the other works available.

The chosen period is one which generally contains events within the memory of a large number of people in Sheffield - this is not a book about crinolines or bowler-hats! Neither is it a work of local history in the normal sense of the term. It has far more to do with entertainment than serious study, but we hope you will agree it is none the worse for that. It is hoped that the following pages will prompt readers' own memories of Sheffield from days gone by.

Change' is relentless and the photographs on the pages in the book serve to remind us of some of them. Memories of Sheffield has been a pleasure to compile. We sincerely hope you enjoy reading it.

Happy memories!

AROUND THE CITY CENTRE

Few photographs could evoke the atmosphere and bustle of Sheffield as we once knew it. The barrows and piled up boxes outside the Sheaf Market (more commonly known as the Rag and Tag); the knots of shoppers dodging between the passing cars; people standing on their doorsteps watching the world go by; the old lorries, cars and trams; the adverts on the hoardings that were once so familiar. And spot the old one-horsepower vehicles on the left of the photograph, which remind us of the gentler age when the city's only traffic pollution could be shovelled up and used on your floribunda! The advertisements alone give us a taste of real nostalgia: Bass, Rowntrees Cocoa, Ewbank carpet sweepers, Bisto, Wills Gold Flake, Players, Bovril, and others which we cannot read. Remember the simple slogan, 'Ahh Bisto!'? Few realise that the name Bisto is itself a hidden slogan, being a rearrangement of the initial letters of 'Browns, Seasons, Thickens In One'. Neat - and composed around 1910.

GOLD
FLAKE
ROWNTREE'S
COCOA
Ewbank
BISTO

87 FARGATE.
THIRD PARTY.
ENGINEERING
EAGLE STAR & BR
INSURANCE COM
FIRE
LIFE
ROYAL EXCHAN
SSURANCE
SON Ltd
POPULAR PRICES
J. LYONS & Co Ltd
J. LYONS & Co Ltd
HIGH CLASS
REFRESHMENTS
AT
POPULAR PRICES
WEAR
TIMPSON'S
BOOTS
WILLIAM TIM
CROSS
BASS
CINEMA HO
LIFE LAUGHS AND ROMANCE AT OXFORD U
MEN OF TO-MORRO
STORY OF Q SHIPS

Left: According to the film critics, the cast of 'Men of Tomorrow' was more interesting than the film, which they labelled as 'a dim comedy'. Released in 1932, the film was already three years old when it came to Cinema House in Fargate. Though not nearly as large as some of the city's cinemas, Cinema House was nevertheless as richly decorated as some of the larger establishments. Cinema House opened in 1913 - the era of silent films, of course - and while many cinemas relied on the services of a pianist, who adapted the music to suit the drama or romance of the film, Cinema House boasted a 12-piece orchestra to provide the accompaniment. Eventually, as with so many of Sheffield's familiar landmarks, Cinema House fell victim to the red pen of the planners and was demolished in the early 1960s for redevelopment.

Left: This Union Street photograph is dated 4 May 1950, and in the background a few people have decided to 'get away from it all' for a while and are setting out for a day in the country or by the sea - though number of the hats and warm coats worn by the day trippers indicates that the weather was not the bucket and spade variety. Parking in the city centre was restricted to 20 minutes in the hour, but drivers may have stayed a bit longer as parking enforcement as we know it today began when traffic wardens first marched onto British streets in 1960.

Above: Four years or so after the war, things are stirring in High Street and constructor's huts are in place on the levelled site of Walsh's department store, which had been built by John Walsh back in 1899. Sheffielders with long memories will never forget 12 December, 1940 - and the empty, burnt out shell of the once magnificent store, the pride of the city, after the night-long air raid. Christmas presents had to be purchased elsewhere that dreadful year.... Building restrictions meant that rebuilding work was slow to get underway, but in May 1953 Sheffield got its brand new Walsh's. But the grandeur of the old department store with its delightful restaurant and orchestra, and its good quality fashions and furnishings, is still remembered by many.

Top right: Driving must have been even more hazardous once darkness fell, for this was 1943 and the wartime blackout restricted drivers to showing a downward directed pinpoint of light. Obstructions were painted white so that they could be seen more easily; the lamp standard in the foreground, for example, which would shed no light on High Street until 1945, and the pillar box outside the National Provincial Bank on the left, have been treated in this way. The edges of the pavement have been marked out in white and the safety

rails in front of the trams (known to most as 'dog catchers') have also been painted. The safety rails were a clever innovation which would have swept dropped parcels, dogs - and the odd human - away from the tram's wheels. The building on the left with the imposing portico was, of course, the offices of the Sheffield Telegraph and Star.

KEEP
LEFT

Comparison with older photographs taken in this same spot in High Street makes us appreciate that in a place where jay walkers at one time abounded, the pedestrians using this crossing on 19th April 1952 were behaving in a very orderly manner! It was the appalling accident statistics which led to the creation of the very first pedestrian crossings, and these were to become a remarkably effective road safety device. Marked out by studs and yellow beacons, the crossings were introduced in 1934, and with a fine disregard for the behaviour common to little boys, the first beacons were made of glass. So many of the glass globes were broken that the design was quickly changed and they were replaced by globes of painted aluminium. The date given for our photograph raises more questions than it answers, as across the country, pedestrian crossings were given their white stripes in 1951, and the beacons became plastic and began to wink in 1952. That being the case, this one was a little behind the times, but it would not have been long before High Street had its fully-equipped zebra crossings.

CENTRAL
JWA 768

Left: Rush hour traffic and a heavy downpour are not the ideal mix of circumstances, and people running to get out of the rain seem to be taking their lives in their hands. Though there are a number of private cars in this shot of the Haymarket, public transport was for the vast majority of people the only way to get home after work. For this was 1946 - a year after peace was declared - and a family car was an undreamed of luxury. Spot one of the wooden temporary shops which were hastily built to provide premises for some of the bombed-out businesses.

Below: Queues have formed inside the tram stops in Fitzalan Square back in 1950. Appropriately, the square today is the hub of the new tramway system - a direct echo of the old days, the Supertram having brought us full circle. The Burtons building, in the left background, was badly damaged in the blitz, and stood derelict for many years. The stony gaze of King Edward VII - eldest son of Queen Victoria and Prince Albert - surveys the scars of war which still remain in Fitzalan Square in 1950.

Traffic holdups are not a 21st century phenomenon, as this memorable old photograph reveals! This line of slow moving traffic in London Road (impeded somewhat by Davy's delivery van, which was being unloaded at the time) was recorded on 5th October 1949. The number of small shops in the shot is interesting; remember the time when small grocers like Gallons were a common sight around Sheffield? Sadly, many of them are gone, together with the personal service we once took for granted.

Above: Well into the 1950s the old pre-war cars were in the majority on Sheffield's roads, but those who could afford to buy new vehicles were finding by the middle of the decade that car designs were beginning to change. Mudguards and running boards like those on the 'sit up and beg' design of the old pre-war cars were set to become a thing of the past. This nostalgic view of London Road captures two delivery vans outside Davy's. Which of our older readers cannot remember Davy's legendary cornish pasties and pork pies? And their tomato sausages? Marvellous with a rasher of bacon and a couple of fried eggs! Adjoining Davy's was W E James & Co, where the keen gardener could buy anything from a bag of tulip bulbs to a draw hoe.

Window shopping with a difference was offered at Atkinsons back in September 1950. The air raids of December 1940 turned much of The Moor into a wasteland of rubble, twisted metal and smoke-blackened walls leaning at crazy angles. Atkinson's department store was totally destroyed that night; the next morning revealed a scene of devastation - the roof, walls, windows, floors and all the stock had completely gone. The site was eventually cleared and levelled, but five years after the war had ended vast areas of Sheffield still needed to be rebuilt. Atkinson's had reconstructed display windows but the rebuilding of the store still lay in the future. One of Sheffield's few family firms, Atkinson's new store was eventually reconstructed on its original site. Advertisements are as much part of our nostalgic glimpse through time as the buildings they appeared on, and readers will remember the familiar ad for Goodyear tyres. Back in the 1950s few motorists concerned themselves too much over the amount of tread on their tyres. A decade on, however, this aspect of road safety had become a matter of public concern. When Barbara Castle brought in the first tyre law in the mid 1960s, specifying the minimum legal depth of tread which a tyre must have, tyre sales rocketed.

GOODYEAR
The world's
first choice
Willsons
JOHN ATKINSON
RESTAURANT

Below: Wilson Peck in the left foreground was the music store in Sheffield, and more than a few of our readers will have rocked around the clock to the records they bought there! Our photograph was taken in the late 1950s, when rock 'n' roll was the new music favoured by the young. The parents of the aforementioned young who were true music lovers might also have visited the store and splashed out on a good radiogram or even a piano.

Bottom right: Apart from public transport there was little traffic around in Moorhead when this view was recorded in 1939, and the prominently displayed notice on a tram standard which warns motorists that the standing limit for unoccupied motor cars is 20 minutes would appears to be quite unnecessary. Behind the oncoming tram lay the Nelson Hotel - an establishment which, thirty years or so on, was to have a tragic murder committed on the premises. The Nelson was completely rebuilt in 1963, when its interesting architecture was swept away to make way for a building which was typical of the 'square block' designs which were favoured among the architects of the day. The aforementioned crime took place in the late 1960s, and the pub was at the time still the Nelson. It was later renamed The Hind, and still more recently it went through yet another name change, becoming Seamus O'Donnells.

'No Waiting' warn the signs which sprouted across the city during the 1960s to keep motorists off the streets, and on the day this view was captured in March 1965, not a single driver was around to challenge authority. The Moor - seen here from Young Street - was in fact quite car-free, and the young mother with her baby, and the few shoppers who were about, need have no fear of crossing the road. Milletts' three display windows are crammed with goods; wouldn't it be fascinating to be able to see the prices and compare them with today's? Back in the 1960s, denim jeans had already become entrenched as the fashion of the decade - though they were in fact to remain popular right up to the end of the 1990s. Levi Strauss began to manufacture jeans in the 19th century, mostly for gold miners, and interestingly, they added the now-familiar rivets as reinforcements to stop the weight of the gold nuggets tearing the pockets.

A few passers-by in Union Street are occupied by affairs other than the Victorian splendour of the Newton Chambers Showrooms, and would rarely if ever stop to admire the ornate building with its showy domes and flamboyant architecture. Love it or hate its lavish style, the building was in fact part of the city's history; it was constructed in 1893, and as readers will perhaps already know, its claim to fame was that it was the first iron framed building to be built in Sheffield. About to become part of Sheffield's redevelopment area, Union Street wears an air of desolation and impermanence. The old showrooms were about to be developed by the Boden Group as a store and office building; Newton Chambers had a vast industrial complex at Thornecliffe, near Chapeltown. Name anything in iron, from gates and railings to gas pipes, and Bodens could come up with the goods. Our photograph was dated 1968, and future years would see many changes, not least the nearby roundabout in Furnival Gate.

P
AFTER 5 PM ONLY
T. HASTINGS
CHAPMAN

This marvellous view of Castlefolds fruit and vegetable market dates back to the 1930s. As we can see, there are a number of lorries and cars around but the preference with a number of these traders was obviously the good old horse and cart. The old fashioned method of transport had fewer breakdowns, emitted no pollution apart from the useful used fodder in place of petrol and returned your affection! We might assume that these traders were unloading goods to sell in the market, but they were just as likely to have been loading up with stock to take out on to the roads and sell around the residential areas. An old three wheeled truck takes up much of the foreground; affectionately known as the mechanical horse, these wagons were indeed a useful workhorse. This one belonged to the LMS. The covered part of Castlefolds Market can be seen in the left background; a memorable view, this, as the market was closed in the late 1950s and became part of Parkway Wholesale Market. The Norfolk Market Hall, built in 1851 at a cost of around £40,000, dominates the right background.

Above: It was wartime when this view of the Wicker was captured for posterity. Though some damage was done at the Wicker Arches, these buildings survived the blitz. A number still stand today, among them the Grosvenor Hotel on the left of the photograph, taken on 24 August, 1943. A large sign outside The Grosvenor tells us that this is a Gilmours house. Duncan Gilmour's & Company was founded around 1830, at first as a wines and spirits merchant. Thirty years on, they moved into brewing and were based at Furnival Brewery in Furnival Gate. Our view takes in other interesting buildings: standing taller than the adjoining properties on the right approaching the Wicker Arches (which can just about be seen in the background) is the headquarters of Samuel Osborne & Co, steel manufacturers, today the Sheffield & District Afro-Caribbean Community Association.

Above: The 7 November, 1953, signalled another shopping day in the Haymarket, and the usual buzz of pedestrians in our shot keeps the police officer busy. Some of these eager people, shopping bags in hand, would have been making for Woolworths, where the food was good and the prices affordable, both in the cafe and all around the store. This branch of Woolworths was eventually closed and a new building constructed not too far away, which was opened in 1961. The new Woolworths was built on the site of the old Norfolk Market Hall, and older Sheffielders still have a soft spot for the old market.

Though passers by are wearing coats and caps, a row of open windows in the Town Hall inform us that though this might not have been the warmest day, a little fresh air was nevertheless still needed. Sheffield's Town Hall was built rather later than those of other northern cities; Sheffield had other, more pressing demands on the public purse at the time. However, the land was obtained in 1886, and a competition for the best design was launched. Of the 178 entries the design of Mr E W Mountford was chosen, and 21 May, 1897, was a red letter day for the city when Queen Victoria herself came along to declare the new Town Hall officially open. The magnificent building has lost none of its excellence with the passing of time - its 210ft tower, topped with a very appropriate seven-foot figure of Vulcan, the god of fire, is as much appreciated today as then. Each of its four clock faces measures an incredible 8ft 6in in diameter. To the left of the photograph is the Albany Temperance Hotel, beloved in time gone by among Sheffield's visitors from overseas, today it is the premises of the Yorkshire Bank.

Below: Fashions come and go, but it is doubtful whether teenagers will ever again wear the white ankle socks and sensible shoes worn by the young girl in our photograph! Yet as recently as the 1950s, girls of up to 15 wore socks without batting an eyelid. It was an accepted part of life - especially when it came to school uniform - and nobody stopped to question it. It was not until they were around 15 or 16 years of age that girls would be allowed to wear stockings, at least at the weekend. To the right, above the trams, we can see the Norfolk Market Hall. The market hall was built by the Duke of Norfolk on the site of the old Tontine Inn.

Below right: A service as rare as hen's teeth in our city today - a parking attendant who directs the motorist to an empty space! This particular car park made temporary use of the site of the old Corn Exchange - destined to become the Park Square roundabout. Built by the Duke of Norfolk in 1881, fire destroyed the Corn Exchange in 1947. The building stood, however, for 17 years until it was eventually demolished and the land levelled not long before this scene was recorded in 1964, in readiness for the city's ambitious road building scheme. The solid building in the left background was at one time W H Smith's wholesale premises, later becoming the headquarters of South Yorkshire Passenger Transport Executive. The premises of the Canal Wharf and Warehouses can be seen in the right background, while on the far horizon, tower blocks stand out against the sky.

Left: The date of our photograph is the late 1950 and Gerrards, the well known furriers on the right of our High Street photograph, still had to operate from the ground floor of their building, having lost the upper floors in the blitz ten years earlier. This was of course a number of years before the tide of public opinion swung violently against the wearing of fur; which was still very much a fashion statement in the 1950s, though thankfully few collars were seen still bearing the head of the unfortunate animal! But faux was the way to go, and 20 years on lay the heyday of 'fun fur'.

Below: These fine buildings in Leopold Street mercifully escaped the red pen of the planning department and still survive today. Firth College, on the right - named for the Sheffield industrialist and one-time Mayor Mark Firth - was Hallam University's forerunner. The College was opened back in 1879 by Prince Leopold, the eighth child of Queen Victoria and Albert, the Prince Consort. Part of Orchard Street, where the College stood, was renamed Leopold Street in the Prince's honour. The old Central Grammar School next to Firth College was probably still open at the time of the photograph - 1952. A Number 60 bus bound for Fulwood waits at the bus shelters outside the College to pick up passengers.

Above: Standing proudly against the skyline is the 210ft tower of the Town Hall. Opened on 21 May ,1897, by Queen Victoria, the building's exterior walls were constructed with Stoke Stone from Grindleford, Derbyshire. The architecture of the Town Hall is heavy with symbolism; Two 36ft-long sculpted friezes depict aspects of Sheffield's industry, while representations of Electricity and Steam decorate the main entrance arch.

Right: The busy centre of Attercliffe has long been known as a fine and busy shopping centre, and our mid 1940s photograph includes two of its larger, well known stores. On the left in Attercliffe Road is Littlewoods Department Store; the large chain store was started by Liverpool's Sir John Moores, one-time chairman of Everton FC. In the top left corner of the photograph you will perhaps recognise John Banners department store - and you may already be aware of the store's claim to fame. For the benefit of those who are not, we can repeat that Banners was one of the earliest shops to install escalators for the convenience of its customers.

Above: Eagle eyed readers will perhaps be able to identify the premises of Wigfall & Son Ltd in the background of this Attercliffe shot. The sign above the window tells us that this was their furniture department, but in actual fact you could buy or rent just about anything from Wigfalls, including their inexpensive cycles, (made, according to the local humorists, from surplus gas piping!). Wigfalls - affectionately known, you will remember, as 'Wiggies' - were one of the first stores to get into television rental back in the 1950s; you could also purchase goods on hire purchase, and countless young couples furnished their home courtesy of Wiggies and their 'never never' facilities!

ROYAL LONDON

Left: The splendid Victorian Yorkshire Penny Bank, on the right, was built in 1888-89. The Temperance movement was in full swing by the mid 1800s, and sharing the massive building with the bank was the Albany Hotel, an alcohol free establishment, whose main entrance was in Surrey Street. With the closure of the hotel in 1958 came a number of changes: not only was the building converted to offices, but its rather nice dormer windows and chimneys were removed and replaced with a piece of modern architecture. Adjoining the bank is Carmel House, the premises of the YMCA, who later moved out of the city centre. Its huge Schweppes sign was a familiar sight for many years, though during the 1960s there was no need to mention the company's name - all you had to say was 'you know who...' - and you knew who!

Left: This bank on the corner of London Road and Cemetery Road, together with the surrounding properties, took a real battering during the second of Sheffield's wartime air raids. Well into the 1950s, many damaged properties still lay derelict, while empty plots of land around the city reminded us of the shops and houses that had once stood there. The bank, however, was rebuilt - though future years were to see a dramatic change in the use of the building. Today's customers are not queuing to pay in cheques or use cash machines; Roman candles, rockets and silver fountains are on offer these days at the Chinese fireworks company who now occupy the premises. The Sheffield and Ecclesall Co-op with its marvellous arcade lay across the road at the time of the photograph.

Below: A busy day in the Haymarket, and interestingly this busy junction demands the services of two police officers to cope with the volume of traffic and the large numbers of shoppers. The date was 22 July, 1961, and the shot includes some of the popular vehicles of the day such as the Standard 10 in the right foreground - and spot the Morris J4 van on the right. Sheffield's changeover to motor buses has been made at the time of the photograph, though the tramlines still remained. The old rails still come to light from time to time when our ever present road works unearth them. Woolworths new store was under construction when this scene was recorded, and a long length of hoarding separates the building work from the many pedestrians. Directly opposite was Davy's, on the corner of Castle Street, and the well-

known gents outfitters Weaver to Wearer in the adjoining premises - a favoured place to buy your suits, shirts and sports jackets.

Above: A sunny April day at Cole's corner, and pedestrians who have somewhere to go stride out to get there. The young man in the foreground looks as though he's bound for Bakewell! So busy was this crossing that two police officers were needed. Why, we wonder, did one have a white coat and the other not? Facing us is Kingdon's tobacconist's, a dying breed today. Back in 1952, the date of our photograph, however, there were many tobacconists dotted around the city, often stocking sweets and chocolate as well as cigarettes.

Below: Motor cycle enthusiasts will immediately spot the distinctive fish-tail exhaust pipe on what is almost certainly a Velocette LE. And what about the gear the rider is wearing? How things have changed since 1953, when motor cyclists were not obliged to wear safety helmets! Today's emphasis is far more geared towards safety, and riders are well protected by their leathers and helmets, which come in many different colours. The Haymarket was as busy as usual, and the lady on the left is looking to dodge between the cars and the oncoming trams and get across the road. The date was 7 November, 1953, and the day was obviously a cool one judging by the coats, caps and headscarves we can spot in the crowd.

Right: After dark Sheffield comes to brilliant life with hundreds of coloured lights that sparkle like gems in the darkness. The old 'hole in the road' looks special in this Yuletide view, which was caught on film in 1967 soon after it was opened. The open topped subway in High Street was officially named Castle Square, though just about everyone called it simply 'the hole in the road'. Is there any truth in the rumour, we wonder, that the subway - today the Castle Square Supertram stop - was filled in with rubble from Hyde Park flats? The area is quite unrecognisable since Arundel Gate was laid down and so many modern buildings constructed.

Right: There was a time when high streets around the country were sprinkled with an assortment of different shoe shops: True-Form, Freeman, Hardy and Willis, Saxone, Dolcis, Timpson, Stead and Simpson, Barratts, - there they all were. Is it imagination, or are there fewer shoe shops about today? Some of these well-known independent stores are, of course, still with us, though others perhaps have been swallowed up by the larger chains. Adjoining True-Form at the time was Woolworths, and a prominent sign advertises their cafeteria - a popular place for a shopper's snack on Saturday lunchtimes.

True-For
OOLWORTH
AFETERIA
4
BENTS GREEN
7440 WJ

ON THE BIG SCREEN

Right: This was the old Cinema House in Fargate back in 1932. The effects of national depression were still being felt - in fact as late as 1939 two million were still on the dole. Every now and again it was possible, however, to scrape a few coppers together for a visit to the pictures, and 'Rookery Nook' and Conan Doyle's 'The Missing Rembrandt' were being shown at Cinema House when this revealing scene was captured for us. Only a couple of years earlier Cinema House had shown the film 'Climbing the Golden Stair'; not only was this the cinema's first talking picture, but it was also shown in colour - a great innovation at the time.

Far right: 'An old fashioned heartwarmer' was how critics described the film 'Lassie Come Home'. Though only Roddy McDowall got a mention on the canopy above the Rex Cinema's doorways, a very young Elizabeth Taylor also appeared in the film, enchanting audiences everywhere and making her indelible mark on the cinema-going public. The Rex, on the corner of Mansfield Road and Hollybank Road, was built to seat 1,350 - an ideal size during the heyday of the cinema, but over-large when the influence of television began to take its toll of cinema audiences. The Rex closed at the end of 1982 with 'Gregory's Girl' and Chariots of Fire'.

CINEMA
RODDY MC DOWALL IN LASSIE COME HOME

These photographs of Fitzalan Square will give readers a nostalgic trip down Memory Lane. The News Theatre (right) sits cosily - though differing greatly in style - between the imposing Barclays Bank building on the one side and the Bell Hotel - a Tetley's House - on the other. The site of the News Theatre had been associated with entertainment since the turn of the century, when displays of animated pictures were shown at an establishment known as Wonderland. In 1911, the Electra Palace cinema was opened, and the design of the building, its innovative facilities, and its imaginative programmes, established it as a firm favourite with cinema-goers. There was no need to

of the continuous shows which were to gain much popularity in later years. The Electra Palace closed in July 1945 and opened around six weeks later as a Capital and Provincial News Theatre. Perhaps this view was captured during the school holidays in the early 1950s - a Disney film and the Tom and Jerry Cartoons advertised would hold particular appeal for the kiddies. In a time when television was still a novelty to the vast majority of people, the News Theatres which sprang up around the country a decade earlier quickly gained popularity. People kept in touch with what was going on in the world - particularly relevant during the war - through the newsreels which were shown continuously from three in the afternoon until 19.30 at night. A night out at the pictures was a popular pastime during the 1930s and 40s - in fact in 1939 an incredible twenty million British people went to the cinema every week. Television became a way of life during the 1950s, and sadly the writing was on the wall for many of our popular cinemas. The News Theatre found its services redundant and in January 1962 it reopened as the Classic cinema (left).

miss any of the programme; not only could audiences take afternoon tea in the first floor lounge, but people could if they wished have refreshments brought to them in their seats! The Electra introduced a 'come when you please, leave when you please' policy - the first

In the 1950s the choice of cinemas for the people of Sheffield was wide, and in the days when people went to the pictures several times a week they were all well patronised. Our nostalgic photograph will bring back memories of Barker's Pool as it was in 1952, when the Gaumont and Cinema House faced each other across the busy main road. The elegant white tower and striking dome of the Cinema House had been a well known landmark in the city since the cinema was built back in 1913, when silent films were the only option.

Though experimental displays of sound equipment were mounted, Cinema House was one of the last in the city to install the new technology. Its first talking picture, ‘Climbing the Golden Stair’, was shown in February 1930. The Gaumont - huge in contrast with the 800-seat Cinema House - opened in 1927 as The Regent. The newer of the two cinemas converted to sound in June 1929, and charged no extra for its screening of ‘Show Boat’, starring Laura La Plante and Joseph Schildkraut.

Right: The foyer of the Gaumont was ablaze with light, though Barkers Pool was empty of pedestrians when this view was caught on camera in the Christmas of 1960. The Town Hall clock informs us that the time is 5.35pm, so we can assume that most people are on their way home after a long day at the office. The cinema started life as The Regent back in 1927, and the opening programme included a concert as well as the screening of 'My Best Girl', which starred everyone's sweetheart, Mary Pickford. The Gaumont lost its battle for life in 1985, and it was demolished to make way for a controversial new cinema and shopping complex. Who can ever forget Prince Charles' 'carbuncle on the face of Sheffield' comment which set the cat running loose among the pigeons? Many would agree with the heir to the throne's poor opinion of the new development, while others argue in its favour, praising its imaginative design.

Below: A row of taxis outside the Picture House in Barkers Pool are waiting for the lucky few who are enjoying a night out at the cinema - a seasonal treat, perhaps, judging by the twinkling Christmas tree near the cinema. 'High Noon' so this picture dates from around 1952 when the film starring Gary Cooper and Grace Kelly was first released.

GAUMON
RESTAURANT

Right: A fairly unmemorable programme was playing at the Odeon in Norfolk Street when a photographer recorded this scene for posterity; Rock Hudson was cast opposite Paula Prentiss in 'Man's Favourite Sport', while 'Tammy and the Doctor' was the 'B' movie. The date of the photograph is 1964, and the stiletto heels and knee length skirts among the passers by were typical of the fashion of the day, and the Morris Minor was a popular car of the decade. The Odeon has an interesting history. The partly built post war edifice (which was actually begun in 1939 and postponed for the duration of the war) had to be demolished, redesigned and completely rebuilt owing to the city's plans for a new ring road. The new Odeon provided seating for 2,340 on two levels and its crimson velvet seats, wall to wall carpeting, comfortable sofas and the latest sound and projection technology. The new cinema opened on 16th July 1956 - and closed again in June 1971, going 'eyes down' to Bingo the very next day.

Right: The X-rated 'Blood is my Heritage' and 'Teenage Frankenstein' were playing at the Wicker Picture House when our photograph was taken in March 1958. The Wicker opened as a cinema in 1920, though stage shows as well as films were put on by the management. The success of moving pictures was by no means assured back then, and it was as well to have more than one horse in the race, just in case! Failure, however, was not on the agenda. People flocked to view the modern miracle, and they were prepared to pay the high price of 9d for a seat on the ground floor. The Wicker came through the wartime air raids - though not unscathed, and survived both flood and fire. It went through several renovations in its long life, and became Studio 7 in 1974 - but closed its doors for the last time on 20 August, 1987.

GAUMONT
THE REGENT
RESTAURANT
FOOTWEAR
DAINTIES
KEEP LEFT

Thirty years separate our two views of the Gaumont Cinema in Barker's Pool, and the contrasting shots show the changes and modernisations which had been made during the intervening years. There were not as many as one might have imagined - though the 1952 view retains the cinema's original name The Regent. Built in the days before talking pictures, The Regent was opened on 26 December, 1927. The cinema had a good-sized stage, a number of dressing rooms and a Wurlitzer organ as well as a screen and projection equipment, and live shows could be staged as well as films. The Regent and The Central screened Sheffield's very first talking pictures on the same evening. It is difficult for those born into this age of technology to understand exactly what an impact sound had on the cinema-going public - this was a mind-blowing step forward! Though very simply designed on the outside, The Regent's interior was comfortable and luxurious. The Regent was renamed the Gaumont as early as 1946, and survived the advent of the silver screen in the corner of everyone's lounge by twinning and then tripling its premises in 1969 and 1979 under the Rank organisation. It showed its last films in November 1985 before being demolished and replaced with the controversial development we know today.

How many of our readers remember the many pleasant hours spent at the Classic Cinema in Fitzalan Square (right) - possibly followed by a good Sheffield curry at the Indus Restaurant? (Remember its familiar genie logo?) The cinema started life as the Electra Palace back in 1911, and the building's elegant facade won the praise of many for its imaginative design. When talking pictures became the latest technology, the management of the Electra Palace was swift to install the necessary equipment, and on 6 January, 1930, they opened the doors on their very first sound movie, 'Movietone Follies of 1929'. The cinema was the last word in luxury, with roses and greenery arranged tastefully at the front of the auditorium, plush tip-up seats, imaginative decor, cleverly placed electric lighting and stained glass windows. As the second world war ended the cinema closed for renovations and a change of use, and on 8th September 1945 it reopened as the News Theatre - which many readers will remember. By the 1960s, television had given us ready access to the news, and the News Theatre went through yet more alterations and renovations. This time, the ornate facade which had become a familiar landmark in the city disappeared behind typical 1960s-design cladding, and the Classic Cinema was born, its huge logo informing passers-by that it was 'the best any time'.

When our view below was captured on the 26 November, 1982, the Classic, part of the Cannon group, had already closed its doors to audiences for the last time. The final film, 'Rocky III' had been shown two days earlier, and the building already wore an air of desolation. Subsequent attempts were made to make this a listed building - an honour it surely deserved - but the pleas of campaigners fell on deaf ears. For two more years the Classic slowly decayed until fire swept through the old cinema on 15 February, 1984, putting a final end to any thought of preservation (below). The burnt-out building was later demolished.

MEMORABLE MOMENTS

Thousands of pounds worth of damage was caused, and scores of families were made homeless across 40 square miles when storms lashed South Yorkshire at the beginning of July 1958. In a few short hours the River Sheaf rose an incredible 14 ft, and unable to cope with the force of the torrent, the river banks burst and a wall of water surged into the surrounding streets. The parapet of the road bridge at Totley Brook was completely swept away, followed by a street lamp and a footbridge; cars were picked up like toys and smashed against buildings, and floodwater poured into nearby homes. Clyde Road, Heeley, was one of the worst hit by the pent up force of the flood water (left). The upper floors were the only answer as people realised that they were trapped in their homes, and the bedrooms became a refuge for entire families. When the flood water eventually subsided, wet, hungry and mud spattered people ventured out to assess the damage. Indoors, their carpets and linoleum were covered with a thick layer of silt and mud; wallpaper was stained with dirty tide marks which showed just how high the water had reached, while television sets, sideboards, tables and three piece suites were completely ruined. Our photographs reveal a little of what lay outside, where the road was still awash with mud and debris - and the hard-pressed fire brigade was called upon to pump away hundreds of gallons of flood water that had turned roads into lakes. Neighbours helped each other to drag their soggy possessions out on to the pavements. It was all too much for some of the children who lived in the area; the camera has caught a look of sad bewilderment on the face of one little girl. What clothes and toys did she lose in that traumatic night, we wonder?

Above: It was back in 1937 when an enterprising photographer snapped this busy scene in the Haymarket from the Brightside and Carbrook Co-op (destined, sadly, to be destroyed a few years later in the Blitz). The date was 22 May, and on the left of the photograph we can see the garlands and bunting still

garden sheds, greenhouses and garages - some complete with cars - and uprooting trees . One elderly lady was warned by neighbours in the nick of time before her cottage in Yarborough Road crumbled under the onslaught and fell into the river. When daylight came the full extent of the damage was revealed. A number of families were left homeless, without food, and with only the clothes they were wearing, and many of them found refuge in Fir Vale Infirmary. The Women's Voluntary Service, as it was then, and the Sheffield Lions Club, were just two of the organisations which rolled up their sleeves and came to the rescue. Dry clothing was a priority, and an urgent appeal went out for help.

hanging from the buildings, celebrating the coronation of King George VI. With all manor of motorised transport trying to negotiate a safe passage along the road, and people in the middle of the road boarding trams, it is hard to imagine how accidents did not occur on a regular basis.

Above and right: It was 2 July, 1958, - the height of the British summer time - and though the odd thunderstorm could be expected, the catastrophic effects of this particular storm caught South Yorkshire unawares. As the River Sheaf burst its banks in the night of disastrous flooding, many Sheffield families had to abandon their homes to the water and spend the night in hastily arranged reception centres. In some areas, thousands of gallons of water surged through streets and gardens, sweeping away

Left and below: Sheffield turned out in full force to welcome King George VI and Queen Elizabeth when they visited the city on 25 September, 1945. In Broomhill hundreds of people lined the route of the royal couple's procession, and eager anticipation can be seen on every face. Union Jacks hang from upper windows - and when the royal car arrives, the same windows will no doubt give a few lucky people a convenient

grandstand view! Fortunately, the weather was fine and the hood of the King and Queen's limousine was let down, giving the crowds a good view of the royal couple. The purpose of their visit was to open the new Ladybower Reservoir (which had actually been planned 46 years earlier), where King George ceremonially turned a wheel, sending water through the outlet valves. The 504 acre reservoir, which would supply water to Nottingham, Leicester and Derby as well as Sheffield, could hold up to 6,300,000,000 gallons.

Right: When women tie scarves around their hair, roll up their sleeves and bring out the buckets, mops and cleaning cloths, it spells curtains for any dirt and grime that happens to be around. Not a crisp bag, not a sweet wrapper - not even a spent match - lie around Darnall railway station to mar its smart appearance; the posts have been whitewashed, the seats dusted, and any brave dandelion or daisy that has dared to raise its head among the colourful blooms in the flowerbeds has been ruthlessly uprooted. And as the photographer records the occasion for posterity, even the Darnall Station sign is being treated to a final polish. If readers are wondering what prompted such a level of care and attention we can reveal. The year was 1962, and final preparations were being made for the 'Best Kept Station' competition. The ladies' loving care paid off, as Darnall, of course, very deservedly ran away with the award.

THE PEOPLES WAR

Below: Looking extremely fetching in dungarees and tin hats, the Central Library staff get together for a group photograph. This was 1940, and the buckets and stirrup pumps placed near them on the library roof hint at the fact that the girls were going through their ARP training at the time. The 16-strong group is 100 per cent female - not unusual for wartime, as many of their husbands, sweethearts and brothers had already joined up, left their jobs, and gone to war.

As they had in the previous war, women took over their jobs in machine shops and engineering factories, turning out armaments and aeroplane parts, driving buses and lorries - in fact doing most kinds of work that had always been looked on as 'jobs for the boys'. Housewives across the country discovered talents and abilities they never knew they had, and developed skills which surprised even themselves.

Above: The inevitable knot of spectators gather to watch as the RAF prepare to inflate their barrage balloon on Crookemoor Recreation Ground, one of the 72 sites which had been earmarked for these all important defences during World War II. Note the gas cylinders piled in readiness on the trailer behind the lorry, most probably containing helium. Parks and other areas of open land made ideal sites for the balloons, which were an effective obstacle to the kind of dive bombing raids sometimes made by the enemy. The city clocked up a total of 130 air raid alerts during the war. Every one of the 72 barrage balloons was up and flying during the blitz, and even though 47 of them were damaged in the raids, they were immediately repaired and within 12 hours were back on duty.

Below: The barrage balloon on Crookesmoor recreation ground attracted a host of spectators who gawped in awe at the remarkable sight. Balloon squadrons had been formed in May and over 1,000 locals volunteered to serve in them, with operations directed from RAF Norton.

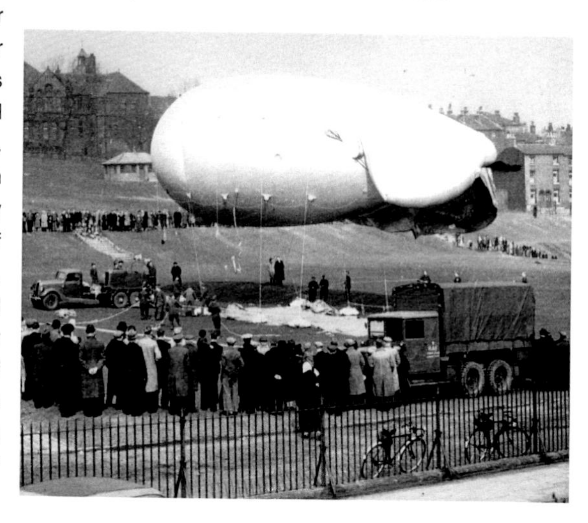

Below: Gas masks were issued to all British civilians at the start of the war as there was a very real fear in Britain that Nazi German bombers would drop poison gas bombs. Babies however, had special cradle-like respirators which would only be issued if an emergency situation arose. Babies were put inside the case and when all the covering flaps were folded and the straps closed up. The baby was totally enclosed and fresh air was pumped in, using a hand pump, through a filter on the side ensuring the infant inhaled no gas.

Above: Seen here in 1939, are two small boys in gas masks being guided by a warden. The boys look quite relaxed as they receive instruction, as every effort was made to accustom children to the frightening and claustrphobic gas masks, that made the wearers look like fearsome monsters. Because of the threat of mustard gas attacks, children in particular had regular half hour gas mask drills. The masks, when new, were very stiff and tight and uncomfortable to wear.

Below: It was possibly the acute wartime shortages of food and supplies which made doctors, health workers and mothers alike very aware of the health of the new generation, and children were carefully weighed, measured and immunised against illness, as can be seen in this Child Welfare Clinic picture in 1950. During the war, children had their own ration books which entitled pre-school children to an allowance of cod-liver oil and orange juice. Long before the advent of the cod liver oil capsule, the recommended spoonful of cod liver oil was administered to the youngest children every day. Children might have screwed up their noses at the fishy taste, but the nourishing cod liver oil went a long way towards keeping them healthy.

Below: Even the rescue teams from the civil defence organisations were stunned by the carnage around Fitzalan Square. In their heart of hearts, they knew it was on the cards, but nothing prepared them for the stark reality of the destruction wreaked by the German bombers that struck during the night of 12-13 December 1940. Sheffield manufactured munitions, armour plate and aircraft parts for the military and was a strategic target for the enemy. The night that Sheffield will never forget was cloudier than attacking planes liked. They preferred perfect vision and a full moon, but low cloud hung over the city. The first wave dropped incendiaries to mark the path for the following planes to dump their loads of high explosive on selected targets below. However, because of the visibility fires were started close to the city centre and not near the factories along the Don valley as intended. People knew what was coming and rushed to take what shelter they could, but death and destruction were inevitable once the bombs started falling.

Above: The civil defence did its best in clearing up after the air raids of 12-13 December 1940, but it was a mammoth task. When the main attack got under way, buildings around Campo Lane and Vicar Lane were flattened, but the most dramatic destruction took place around High Street when the C&A store was blasted by a 1,000 lb bomb. Across the way, the Marples Hotel and neighbouring buildings also suffered extensive damage. Many had taken refuge in the Marples as it had extensive cellars that they presumed would act as a protective air raid shelter. The hotel then took a direct hit an hour after the first strike. A bomb came straight through the roof and detonated at ground floor level, right above the place where frightened staff, guests and members of the public had taken refuge. Somehow, seven men escaped serious injury, but about 70 were killed and that included a number who were never properly identified. Joe Davis, the world billiards and snooker champion was a fortunate man. He was booked to play an exhibition match there that evening, but could not get there as the railway line from Hull had been bombed.

Above: Looking very smart, the York & Lancaster Regiment 69 West Riding Home Guard C-Company stand to attention for inspection. This was the first parade of a Sheffield Home Guard Unit; the men were a credit to the city, and a photographer was present to record the event for posterity. When war broke out in 1939, Sir Anthony Eden, the Secretary of State for War, made a radio appeal for men outside military age to volunteer for membership of the LDV to defend their country in the event of Nazi invasion. Old or young, every member of the LDV was prepared to do his or her bit for Britain. At the beginning of the war, broom handles were typical of the type of 'weapon' the new force had to made improvise with, as arms were in short supply.

Right: It's 'Eyes left!' as a unit of the York and Lancaster Home Guard Regiment march past the saluting base in front of the Town Hall back in 1940. As many readers will remember, military parades were to become an accepted part of life during the second world war, and were a real morale-booster. Remember the far-off beat of the drum which brought us all scurrying out of our houses and down the street to watch the soldiers march by to the rhythm of the rousing bands? The parades undoubtedly made the average person in the street feel in touch with the military and the progress of the war. The Home Guard might have been an amateur force, but they were very well organised.

Below: On the 12 December, 1940, the air raid sirens sounded across Sheffield, signalling a long night of untold destruction as German bombs rained down on the city for hour after hour. Those who worked at C&A Modes Ltd in High Street found this heartbreaking sight awaiting them on their arrival - little remained of the handsome fashion store apart from a smouldering mass of twisted steel girders. Opened in 1932, the building had been built a mere eight years earlier on the site of the old Fitzalan Market. Next door, the Burtons building on the corner of Angel Street was ruined - as were virtually all the buildings on that side of High Street. Strangely, there was little damage done to the premises opposite.

Above: An unbelievable crowd of 20,000 turned out to cheer Prime Minister Winston Churchill when he visited Sheffield on 8 November, 1941. He was able to promise little other than 'blood, sweat and tears', but his stirring speeches inspired the people of Britain in general and Sheffield in particular, and they were with him all the way. As his limousine swept through the city streets, old and young alike cheered him on as he waved his stick, his bowler hat and his big cigar, returning his famous 'V for Victory' sign. Outside the Town Hall vast crowds gathered, yelling, waving, cheering - then listening with respect as he spoke into the microphone, sympathising with the people of Sheffield and berating Adolf Hitler and his policies. After all the city had gone through at the hands of the Luftwaffe, Sheffield needed all the encouragement that the great wartime leader had to give - and they loved him.

Left and above: When VE Day finally arrived the whole country erupted with a mixture of joy and relief. After nearly six years of fighting the Germans it was all over.The desperate days of the blitz were temporarily forgotten in a blaze of flags, fireworks and floodlights. As Martha and the Vandellas said, there was "Dancing in the Street" amidst parties which took place on virtually every street in the city. Trestle tables were dragged out of church halls and schoolrooms as neighbours mucked in together to set up impromptu parties. Celebrations can been seen in full swing in this photograph from one of the parties taking place in Hoyland Street, Wincobank, in May 1945. A full week's rations were used to provide sandwiches, buns, cakes and jugs of lemonade for the children. Dancing to records on an old gramophone, we had not partied like this since the Coronation in 1937.

Powerful childhood memories were forged by the parties which were organised in local communities across the country. This is quite a striking image when you consider that these children in Rushdale Avenue (above inset), are celebrating Victory in Europe by raising a Union Jack flag and preparing to burn an effigy of Hitler.

WHEELS OF TIME

Below: Refuse collecting has never been thought of as the most pleasant job in the world, but alongside the task of these two 'bin men', today's refuse collectors have never had it so good! In a rather nice Sheffield suburb - rubbish is being disposed of in a way which is quite unfamiliar to us today as two brave blokes have a close encounter with cinders, ash, dirt and smells, not to mention climbing the ladder and tip it in. It all went with the job. A third member of the team has been assigned a slightly better duty as the

driver of Dustcart Number 64 - a very strange vehicle. Contrast all this with the marvellous vehicles and their mechanical crushers which the City of Sheffield's Cleansing Department has today, and the gloves, protective clothing, plastic bags and special bins. How times have changed! The photograph was taken around 1940.

Above: Teaching young children to take care on the roads has always formed an important part of police work, and our happy snap, captured some time in the 1960s, records one of those vital road safety events. Acting out the theme with their pedal cars, scooters and dolls' prams made the demonstration fun and taught these youngsters - the drivers of the future - the meaning of various road signs and showed them just how to use pedestrian crossings. How many of our readers will recognise themselves as one of these children and will remember this road safety demonstration?

How many of these jay-walking pedestrians are taking notice of the lone police officer on point duty in Fargate? The neglect was enough to give him a complex! The reason for the huge crowds and air of suppressed excitement seems to have been Cole Brothers sale - the whole world appears to be beating a path to their door. A terrifying barrage of trams has turned Fargate into an obstacle course which makes us all the more thankful that present day planning has created a vehicle-free pedestrianised area, while High Street and Church Street are part of our one-way system.

Below: This scene viewed from a vantage point above the Haymarket, had once been occupied by the Brightside and Carbrook Co-op in Exchange Street. A new co-op had already been built on the corner of Angel Street and Castle Street, and long queues formed outside the new store on the day of their grand opening in 1950. At the time of our photograph, however, many of Sheffield's bomb sites were used for advertising hoardings and parking cars.

Above: Car number 182 may not have been the 'school special' (was there such a thing back in 1956?), but a good number of schoolchildren are among the passengers about to board this Meadowhead tram. These lively youngsters chat cheerfully to the tram driver before boarding car number 182 which at the time was nearing the end of its lifespan.

Left: Bus stations and railway stations go together like fish and chips or cheese and wine - but it is surprising how many cities around Britain have separated these two means of transport by a ten or fifteen minute walk. Fine for taxi drivers, though not good for holiday-makers carrying a couple of heavy suitcases and wheeling a baby buggy. Sheffield, however, is different. Travellers arriving by train had only to walk a short distance from the Midland Station to the bus station in Pond Street. The bus station was actually planned before the second world war, and by the mid 1950s it was ready for a few renovations. Cold, draughty and damp, those open shelters gave little protection from winter winds and driving rain! In 1956 the bus station received a facelift, which added escalators and bridges to the nearby shops.

Below: The photographer has captured an interesting variety of vehicles, from the faithful old trams in the background to the sporty convertible on the left. Caudles, whose van can be seen driving away from the camera, has long been a well-known Sheffield removals firm. Some kind of activity involving a length of electricity cable and two workmen is taking place atop the lorry behind the convertible. The date of the photograph is 1948.

How many readers still have the pennies they laid on the tramlines to be bent by the wheels of Sheffield's last tram? It would be interesting to know just how many of these novel souvenirs still lie forgotten in drawers and boxes around the city! The last of the old trams signalled the end of an era, but older people will never forget boarding their tram on the way home after a long day's work. Sheffield's tramway services never really recovered after World War II, when no fewer than 14 tramcars were destroyed by enemy bombing and the fires that followed. By the mid 1950s the days of the tram were numbered. A week of celebration preceded the demise of the tramway. The 8 October, 1960, was designated as the last day of Sheffield trams, and to say that the day was rather wet would be understating the torrential downpour. At six o'clock in the evening

536 was sent on its last journey to that great tramshed in the sky.... Sheffield, of course, made history as the last industrial city in England to run a tram service. Since then, of course, the South Yorkshire Supertram has added its own flavour to the city streetscene.

the procession of 15 trams left the depot at Tenter Street - and the pouring rain did not stop people from turning out in their thousands to see them off. In the Town Hall Square, floodlit for the occasion, the Transport Band played 'Auld Lang Syne', and the vast crowd joined in the singing as a farewell wreath was placed on the old car's front bumper.

Tinsley tramshed (ironically, Sheffield Bus Museum today) lay just across the road from Thomas Ward's scrapyard, and it was a simple matter to dispatch the old trams to their final destination. Before long, out came the welding torches and car number

ACKNOWLEDGMENTS

The publishers would like to thank Sheffield City Council and Sheffield Central Library - in particular the Local Studies Department.
South Yorkshire Police Press and Public Retations Department.

Thanks are also due to
Peggy Burns who penned the editorial text.